THIS JOURNAL BELONGS TO:

Hidden Cottage Press
www.hiddencottagepress.com

Cover art by Luke Spooner of Carrion House.

ISBN 978-0998912608

MY MICHIGAN BUCKET LIST
an adventure journal

By J.R. Roper

HIDDEN COTTAGE
PRESS

AUTHOR'S NOTE

I made this journal so that you might record your adventures in the great state of Michigan. Rich in beaches, breweries, charming towns, and unique history, Michigan is the place to relax and explore. Visit www.hiddencottagepress.com for relevant website links.

Forego perfection and record your memories and experiences. Write this for you.

~ J.R. Roper

TABLE OF CONTENTS

If you seek a pleasant peninsula, look about you.

~ MICHIGAN'S STATE MOTTO

MI TOP RECOMMENDATIONS

Mackinac Island- Step back in time and enjoy the relaxing beauty. And the fudge. Lots of fudge.

Fort Michilimackinac/Mackinac Bridge/Mackinaw City- Colonial history, an engineering marvel, and great shopping.

Tahquamenon Falls – Hop around the Lower Falls and take in the beauty of the Upper Falls.

Hartwick Pines State Park- Old growth forest and lots of logging history.

Pictured Rocks National Lakeshore- Take the cruise and take in the unique sandstone formations.

Sleeping Bear Dunes National Lakeshore- One of the most beautiful places in America.

Frankenmuth- Little Bavaria and Bronner's Christmas Wonderland.

Henry Ford Museum/Greenfield Village- Cars, trains, and a village of historic buildings.

Grand Haven Beach (at sunset)- The beach and the boardwalk are amazing. Enjoy the sunset, seated on the pier, with a Pronto Pup in hand.

Silver Lake Sand Dunes- Take a dune ride or hike all the way to Lake Michigan. Don't forget a water bottle.

Traverse City- A gorgeous bay, charming town, and fantastic wineries.

Torch Lake- Michigan's longest inland lake known for its clear, turquoise waters.

Bond Falls- An amazing waterfall in the western Upper Peninsula.

Fayette Historic State Park- A restored ghost town in a breathtaking bay.

Isle Royale State Park- A remote island in Lake Superior that is ideal for adventurers who enjoy hiking and rustic camping.

The Soo Locks- Maritime history and engineering.

Porcupine Mountains- Take in the northern majesty.

MY MICHIGAN BUCKET LIST

✔	My destinations.

MY MICHIGAN BUCKET LIST

MY MICHIGAN BUCKET LIST

MY MICHIGAN BUCKET LIST

MY DESTINATION

Destination Details:

Date:

Travel Companions:

Weather:

Recommended Vacation Guides/Maps:

Insider Tips:

Drink & Dine:

To My Surprise:

I Will Never Forget:

My Reflections:

MY DESTINATION

Destination Details:

_____

_____

_____

_____

_____

Date:

Travel Companions:

_____

_____

Weather:

_____

Recommended Vacation Guides/Maps:

_____

Insider Tips:

_____

_____

_____

_____

Drink & Dine:

_____

_____

_____

_____

_____

To My Surprise:

I Will Never Forget:

My Reflections:

MY DESTINATION

Destination Details:

Date:

Travel Companions:

Weather:

Recommended Vacation Guides/Maps:

Insider Tips:

Drink & Dine:

To My Surprise:

I Will Never Forget:

My Reflections:

MY DESTINATION

Destination Details:

Date:

Travel Companions:

Weather:

Recommended Vacation Guides/Maps:

Insider Tips:

Drink & Dine:

To My Surprise:

_____

_____

_____

_____

_____

I Will Never Forget:

_____

_____

_____

_____

_____

My Reflections:

_____

_____

_____

_____

_____

_____

_____

_____

_____

_____

_____

MY DESTINATION

Destination Details:

Date:

Travel Companions:

Weather:

Recommended Vacation Guides/Maps:

Insider Tips:

Drink & Dine:

To My Surprise:
_____
_____
_____
_____
_____

I Will Never Forget:
_____
_____
_____
_____
_____

My Reflections:
_____
_____
_____
_____
_____
_____
_____
_____
_____
_____
_____
_____

MY DESTINATION

Destination Details:

Date:

Travel Companions:

Weather:

Recommended Vacation Guides/Maps:

Insider Tips:

Drink & Dine:

To My Surprise:

I Will Never Forget:

My Reflections:

MY DESTINATION

Destination Details: _____

_____

_____

_____

_____

Date: _____

Travel Companions: _____

_____

Weather: _____

Recommended Vacation Guides/Maps: _____

_____

Insider Tips: _____

_____

_____

_____

Drink & Dine: _____

_____

_____

_____

_____

To My Surprise:

_____

_____

_____

_____

_____

I Will Never Forget:

_____

_____

_____

_____

_____

My Reflections:

_____

_____

_____

_____

_____

_____

_____

_____

_____

_____

_____

MY DESTINATION

Destination Details:

Date:

Travel Companions:

Weather:

Recommended Vacation Guides/Maps:

Insider Tips:

Drink & Dine:

To My Surprise:

I Will Never Forget:

My Reflections:

MY DESTINATION

Destination Details:

_____

_____

_____

_____

_____

Date:

Travel Companions:

_____

_____

Weather:

_____

Recommended Vacation Guides/Maps:

_____

Insider Tips:

_____

_____

_____

_____

Drink & Dine:

_____

_____

_____

_____

To My Surprise:

I Will Never Forget:

My Reflections:

MY DESTINATION

Destination Details:
_____
_____
_____
_____
_____

Date:
_____
Travel Companions:
_____
_____

Weather:
_____

Recommended Vacation Guides/Maps:
_____

Insider Tips:
_____
_____
_____
_____

Drink & Dine:
_____
_____
_____
_____

To My Surprise:
_____
_____
_____
_____
_____

I Will Never Forget:
_____
_____
_____
_____
_____

My Reflections:
_____
_____
_____
_____
_____
_____
_____
_____
_____
_____
_____
_____

Destination Details:

Date:

Travel Companions:

Weather:

Recommended Vacation Guides/Maps:

Insider Tips:

Drink & Dine:

To My Surprise:

I Will Never Forget:

My Reflections:

MY DESTINATION

Destination Details:

Date:

Travel Companions:

Weather:

Recommended Vacation Guides/Maps:

Insider Tips:

Drink & Dine:

To My Surprise:

I Will Never Forget:

My Reflections:

MY DESTINATION

Destination Details:

Date:

Travel Companions:

Weather:

Recommended Vacation Guides/Maps:

Insider Tips:

Drink & Dine:

To My Surprise:

I Will Never Forget:

My Reflections:

Destination Details:

Date:

Travel Companions:

Weather:

Recommended Vacation Guides/Maps:

Insider Tips:

Drink & Dine:

To My Surprise:

I Will Never Forget:

My Reflections:

MY DESTINATION

Destination Details:

_____

_____

_____

_____

_____

_____

Date:

Travel Companions:

_____

_____

Weather:

_____

Recommended Vacation Guides/Maps:

_____

_____

Insider Tips:

_____

_____

_____

_____

_____

Drink & Dine:

_____

_____

_____

_____

_____

To My Surprise:

_____

_____

_____

_____

_____

I Will Never Forget:

_____

_____

_____

_____

_____

My Reflections:

_____

_____

_____

_____

_____

_____

_____

_____

_____

_____

_____

_____

MY DESTINATION

Destination Details:

Date:

Travel Companions:

Weather:

Recommended Vacation Guides/Maps:

Insider Tips:

Drink & Dine:

To My Surprise:

I Will Never Forget:

My Reflections:

Destination Details:

Date:

Travel Companions:

Weather:

Recommended Vacation Guides/Maps:

Insider Tips:

Drink & Dine:

To My Surprise:

I Will Never Forget:

My Reflections:

MY DESTINATION

Destination Details:

_____

_____

_____

_____

Date:

Travel Companions:

_____

Weather:

_____

Recommended Vacation Guides/Maps:

_____

Insider Tips:

_____

_____

_____

Drink & Dine:

_____

_____

_____

_____

To My Surprise:

I Will Never Forget:

My Reflections:

MY DESTINATION

Destination Details:

Date:

Travel Companions:

Weather:

Recommended Vacation Guides/Maps:

Insider Tips:

Drink & Dine:

To My Surprise:

I Will Never Forget:

My Reflections:

MY DESTINATION

Destination Details:

Date:

Travel Companions:

Weather:

Recommended Vacation Guides/Maps:

Insider Tips:

Drink & Dine:

To My Surprise:

I Will Never Forget:

My Reflections:

MY DESTINATION

Destination Details:
_____
_____
_____
_____
_____

Date: _____
Travel Companions: _____
_____

Weather: _____

Recommended Vacation Guides/Maps: _____
_____

Insider Tips: _____
_____
_____
_____

Drink & Dine: _____
_____
_____
_____

To My Surprise:

_____

_____

_____

_____

_____

I Will Never Forget:

_____

_____

_____

_____

_____

My Reflections:

_____

_____

_____

_____

_____

_____

_____

_____

_____

_____

_____

_____

MY DESTINATION

Destination Details:

Date:

Travel Companions:

Weather:

Recommended Vacation Guides/Maps:

Insider Tips:

Drink & Dine:

To My Surprise:

I Will Never Forget:

My Reflections:

Destination Details:

Date:

Travel Companions:

Weather:

Recommended Vacation Guides/Maps:

Insider Tips:

Drink & Dine:

To My Surprise:

_____

_____

_____

_____

I Will Never Forget:

_____

_____

_____

_____

_____

My Reflections:

_____

_____

_____

_____

_____

_____

_____

_____

_____

_____

_____

_____

MY DESTINATION

Destination Details:

Date:

Travel Companions:

Weather:

Recommended Vacation Guides/Maps:

Insider Tips:

Drink & Dine:

To My Surprise:

I Will Never Forget:

My Reflections:

MY DESTINATION

Destination Details:

Date:

Travel Companions:

Weather:

Recommended Vacation Guides/Maps:

Insider Tips:

Drink & Dine:

To My Surprise:

I Will Never Forget:

My Reflections:

Destination Details:

Date:

Travel Companions:

Weather:

Recommended Vacation Guides/Maps:

Insider Tips:

Drink & Dine:

To My Surprise:

I Will Never Forget:

My Reflections:

MY DESTINATION

Destination Details:

Date:

Travel Companions:

Weather:

Recommended Vacation Guides/Maps:

Insider Tips:

Drink & Dine:

To My Surprise:

I Will Never Forget:

My Reflections:

MY DESTINATION

Destination Details:

Date:

Travel Companions:

Weather:

Recommended Vacation Guides/Maps:

Insider Tips:

Drink & Dine:

To My Surprise:

_____

_____

_____

_____

I Will Never Forget:

_____

_____

_____

_____

My Reflections:

_____

_____

_____

_____

_____

_____

_____

_____

_____

_____

_____

Destination Details: _____

_____

_____

_____

_____

Date: _____

Travel Companions: _____

_____

Weather: _____

Recommended Vacation Guides/Maps: _____

_____

Insider Tips: _____

_____

_____

_____

Drink & Dine: _____

_____

_____

_____

To My Surprise:

I Will Never Forget:

My Reflections:

MY DESTINATION

Destination Details:

_____

_____

_____

_____

_____

Date:

Travel Companions:

_____

Weather:

_____

Recommended Vacation Guides/Maps:

_____

Insider Tips:

_____

_____

_____

_____

Drink & Dine:

_____

_____

_____

_____

_____

To My Surprise:

_____
_____
_____
_____
_____

I Will Never Forget:

_____
_____
_____
_____
_____

My Reflections:

_____
_____
_____
_____
_____
_____
_____
_____
_____
_____
_____
_____

MY DESTINATION

Destination Details:

Date:

Travel Companions:

Weather:

Recommended Vacation Guides/Maps:

Insider Tips:

Drink & Dine:

To My Surprise:

I Will Never Forget:

My Reflections:

MY DESTINATION

Destination Details:

Date:

Travel Companions:

Weather:

Recommended Vacation Guides/Maps:

Insider Tips:

Drink & Dine:

To My Surprise:

I Will Never Forget:

My Reflections:

Destination Details:

Date:

Travel Companions:

Weather:

Recommended Vacation Guides/Maps:

Insider Tips:

Drink & Dine:

To My Surprise:

I Will Never Forget:

My Reflections:

MY DESTINATION

Destination Details:

Date:

Travel Companions:

Weather:

Recommended Vacation Guides/Maps:

Insider Tips:

Drink & Dine:

To My Surprise:

I Will Never Forget:

My Reflections:

MY DESTINATION

Destination Details:

_____

_____

_____

_____

_____

Date: _____

Travel Companions: _____

_____

Weather: _____

Recommended Vacation Guides/Maps: _____

_____

Insider Tips: _____

_____

_____

_____

Drink & Dine: _____

_____

_____

_____

_____

To My Surprise:

I Will Never Forget:

My Reflections:

MY DESTINATION

Destination Details:

Date:

Travel Companions:

Weather:

Recommended Vacation Guides/Maps:

Insider Tips:

Drink & Dine:

To My Surprise:

_____

_____

_____

_____

_____

_____

I Will Never Forget:

_____

_____

_____

_____

_____

_____

My Reflections:

_____

_____

_____

_____

_____

_____

_____

_____

_____

_____

_____

_____

_____

_____

MY DESTINATION

Destination Details:

Date:

Travel Companions:

Weather:

Recommended Vacation Guides/Maps:

Insider Tips:

Drink & Dine:

To My Surprise:

I Will Never Forget:

My Reflections:

MY DESTINATION

Destination Details:

Date:

Travel Companions:

Weather:

Recommended Vacation Guides/Maps:

Insider Tips:

Drink & Dine:

To My Surprise:

I Will Never Forget:

My Reflections:

MY DESTINATION

Destination Details:

Date:

Travel Companions:

Weather:

Recommended Vacation Guides/Maps:

Insider Tips:

Drink & Dine:

To My Surprise:

I Will Never Forget:

My Reflections:

Destination Details:

Date:

Travel Companions:

Weather:

Recommended Vacation Guides/Maps:

Insider Tips:

Drink & Dine:

To My Surprise:

I Will Never Forget:

My Reflections:

Destination Details:

Date:

Travel Companions:

Weather:

Recommended Vacation Guides/Maps:

Insider Tips:

Drink & Dine:

To My Surprise:

I Will Never Forget:

My Reflections:

MY DESTINATION

Destination Details:

Date:

Travel Companions:

Weather:

Recommended Vacation Guides/Maps:

Insider Tips:

Drink & Dine:

To My Surprise:

_____

_____

_____

_____

_____

I Will Never Forget:

_____

_____

_____

_____

_____

My Reflections:

_____

_____

_____

_____

_____

_____

_____

_____

_____

_____

_____

MY DESTINATION

Destination Details:

Date:

Travel Companions:

Weather:

Recommended Vacation Guides/Maps:

Insider Tips:

Drink & Dine:

To My Surprise:

_____

_____

_____

_____

_____

I Will Never Forget:

_____

_____

_____

_____

_____

My Reflections:

_____

_____

_____

_____

_____

_____

_____

_____

_____

_____

_____

_____

MY DESTINATION

Destination Details:

Date:

Travel Companions:

Weather:

Recommended Vacation Guides/Maps:

Insider Tips:

Drink & Dine:

To My Surprise:

I Will Never Forget:

My Reflections:

MY DESTINATION

Destination Details:

Date:

Travel Companions:

Weather:

Recommended Vacation Guides/Maps:

Insider Tips:

Drink & Dine:

To My Surprise:

I Will Never Forget:

My Reflections:

Destination Details:

Date:

Travel Companions:

Weather:

Recommended Vacation Guides/Maps:

Insider Tips:

Drink & Dine:

To My Surprise:

I Will Never Forget:

My Reflections:

Destination Details:

Date:

Travel Companions:

Weather:

Recommended Vacation Guides/Maps:

Insider Tips:

Drink & Dine:

To My Surprise:

I Will Never Forget:

My Reflections:

Destination Details:

Date:

Travel Companions:

Weather:

Recommended Vacation Guides/Maps:

Insider Tips:

Drink & Dine:

To My Surprise:

I Will Never Forget:

My Reflections:

MY DESTINATION

Destination Details:

Date:

Travel Companions:

Weather:

Recommended Vacation Guides/Maps:

Insider Tips:

Drink & Dine:

To My Surprise:

_____

_____

_____

_____

_____

I Will Never Forget:

_____

_____

_____

_____

_____

My Reflections:

_____

_____

_____

_____

_____

_____

_____

_____

_____

_____

_____

Destination Details:

Date:

Travel Companions:

Weather:

Recommended Vacation Guides/Maps:

Insider Tips:

Drink & Dine:

To My Surprise:

I Will Never Forget:

My Reflections:

MY DESTINATION

Destination Details:

Date:

Travel Companions:

Weather:

Recommended Vacation Guides/Maps:

Insider Tips:

Drink & Dine:

To My Surprise:

I Will Never Forget:

My Reflections:

MY
DINING

Place Name:

Location:

Date:

Notes:

Place Name:

Location:

Date:

Notes:

Place Name:

Location:

Date:

Notes:

Place Name:

Location:

Date:

Notes:

Place Name:

Location:

Date:

Notes:

Place Name:

Location:

Date:

Notes:

Place Name:

Location:

Date:

Notes:

Place Name:

Location:

Date:

Notes:

Place Name:

Location:

Date:

Notes:

Place Name:

Location:

Date:

Notes:

Place Name:

Location:

Date:

Notes:

Place Name:

Location:

Date:

Notes:

Place Name:

Location:

Date:

Notes:

Place Name:

Location:

Date:

Notes:

Place Name:

Location:

Date:

Notes:

Place Name:

Location:

Date:

Notes:

Place Name:

Location:

Date:

Notes:

Place Name:

Location:

Date:

Notes:

Place Name:

Location:

Date:

Notes:

Place Name:

Location:

Date:

Notes:

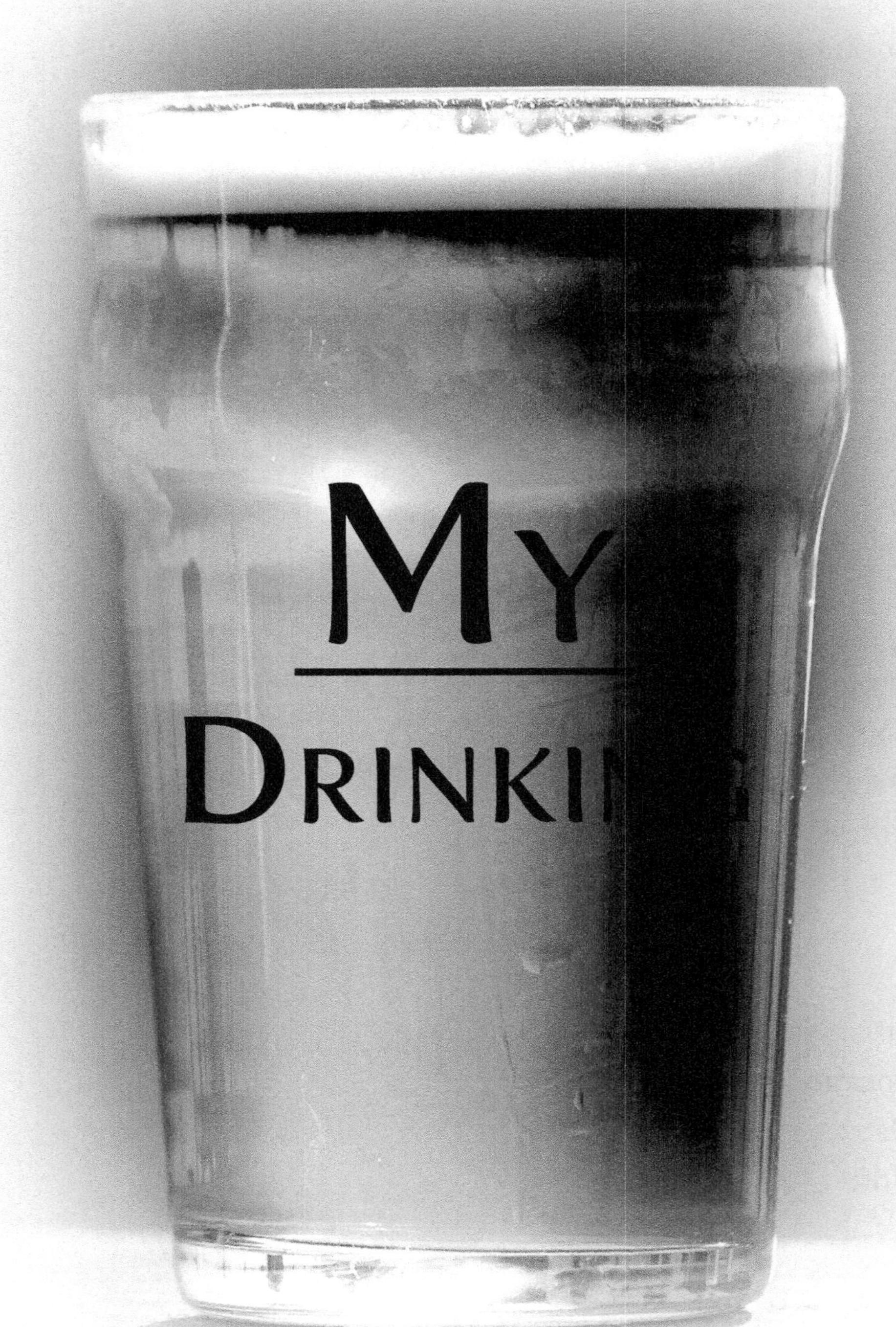
My
Drinki

Place Name:

Location:

Date:

Notes:

Place Name:

Location:

Date:

Notes:

Place Name:

Location:

Date:

Notes:

Place Name:

Location:

Date:

Notes:

Place Name:

Location:

Date:

Notes:

Place Name:

Location:

Date:

Notes:

Place Name:

Location:

Date:

Notes:

Place Name:

Location:

Date:

Notes:

Place Name:

Location:

Date:

Notes:

Place Name:

Location:

Date:

Notes:

Place Name:

Location:

Date:

Notes:

Place Name:

Location:

Date:

Notes:

Place Name:

Location:

Date:

Notes:

Place Name:

Location:

Date:

Notes:

Place Name:

Location:

Date:

Notes:

Place Name:

Location:

Date:

Notes:

Place Name:

Location:

Date:

Notes:

Place Name:

Location:

Date:

Notes:

Place Name:

Location:

Date:

Notes:

Place Name:

Location:

Date:

Notes:

MY
ACCOMMODATIONS

Place Name:

Location:

Date:

Notes:

Place Name:

Location:

Date:

Notes:

Place Name:

Location:

Date:

Notes:

Place Name:

Location:

Date:

Notes:

Place Name:

Location:

Date:

Notes:

Place Name:

Location:

Date:

Notes:

Place Name:

Location:

Date:

Notes:

Place Name:

Location:

Date:

Notes:

Place Name:

Location:

Date:

Notes:

Place Name:

Location:

Date:

Notes:

Place Name:

Location:

Date:

Notes:

Place Name:

Location:

Date:

Notes:

Place Name:

Location:

Date:

Notes:

Place Name:

Location:

Date:

Notes:

Place Name:

Location:

Date:

Notes:

Place Name:

Location:

Date:

Notes:

Place Name:

Location:

Date:

Notes:

Place Name:

Location:

Date:

Notes:

Place Name:

Location:

Date:

Notes:

Place Name:

Location:

Date:

Notes:

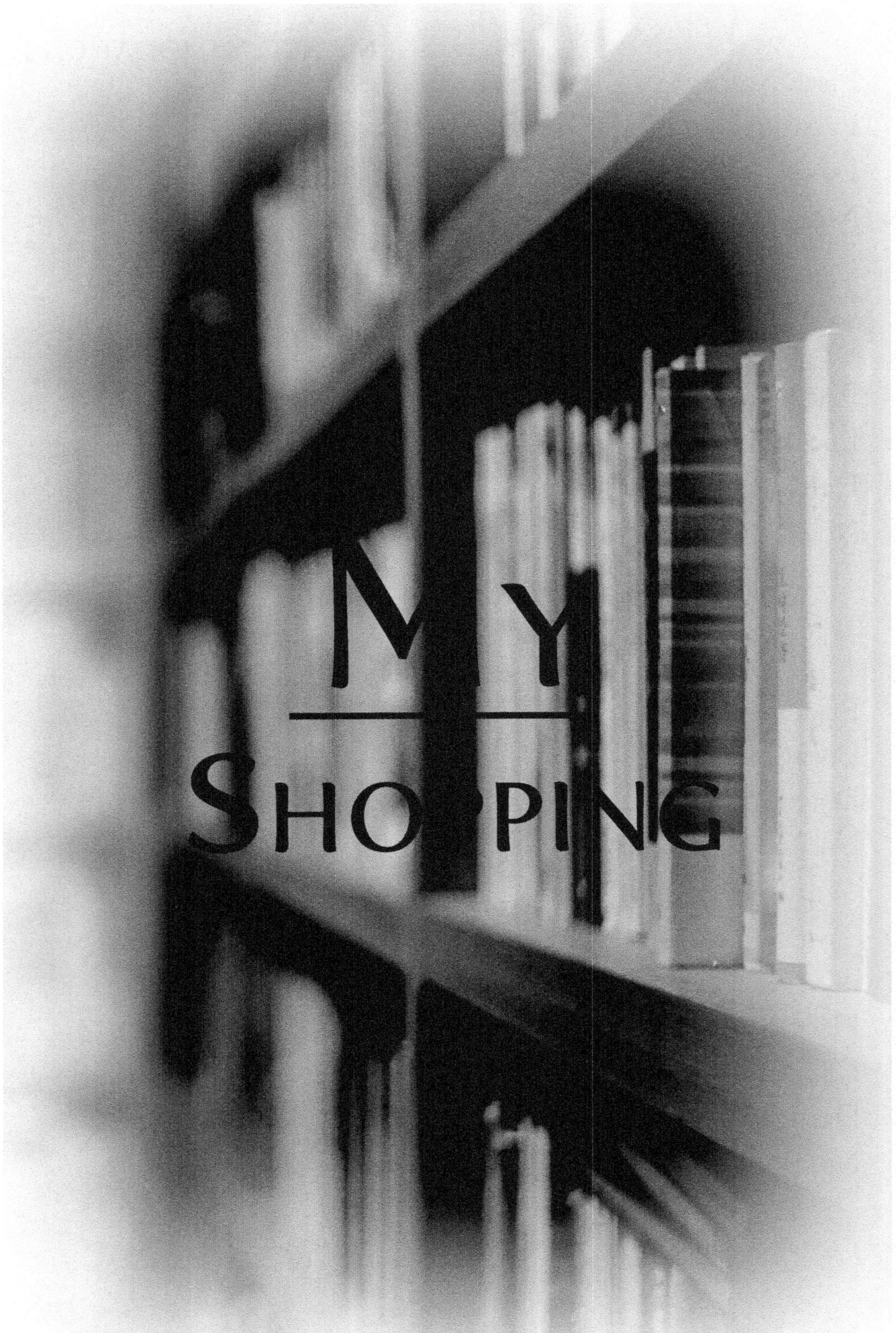
My
Shopping

Place Name:

Location:

Date:

Notes:

Place Name:

Location:

Date:

Notes:

Place Name:

Location:

Date:

Notes:

Place Name:

Location:

Date:

Notes:

Place Name:

Location:

Date:

Notes:

Place Name:

Location:

Date:

Notes:

Place Name:

Location:

Date:

Notes:

Place Name:

Location:

Date:

Notes:

Place Name:

Location:

Date:

Notes:

Place Name:

Location:

Date:

Notes:

Place Name:

Location:

Date:

Notes:

Place Name:

Location:

Date:

Notes:

Place Name: _____

Location: _____

Date: _____

Notes: _____

_____

_____

Place Name: _____

Location: _____

Date: _____

Notes: _____

_____

_____

Place Name: _____

Location: _____

Date: _____

Notes: _____

_____

_____

Place Name: _____

Location: _____

Date: _____

Notes: _____

_____

_____

Place Name:

Location:

Date:

Notes:

Place Name:

Location:

Date:

Notes:

Place Name:

Location:

Date:

Notes:

Place Name:

Location:

Date:

Notes:

MY
HAPPY PLACE

Place Name:

Location:

Date:

Notes:

Place Name:

Location:

Date:

Notes:

Place Name:

Location:

Date:

Notes:

Place Name:

Location:

Date:

Notes:

Place Name:

Location:

Date:

Notes:

Place Name:

Location:

Date:

Notes:

Place Name:

Location:

Date:

Notes:

Place Name:

Location:

Date:

Notes:

Place Name:

Location:

Date:

Notes:

Place Name:

Location:

Date:

Notes:

Place Name:

Location:

Date:

Notes:

Place Name:

Location:

Date:

Notes:

Place Name:

Location:

Date:

Notes:

Place Name:

Location:

Date:

Notes:

Place Name:

Location:

Date:

Notes:

Place Name:

Location:

Date:

Notes:

Place Name:

Location:

Date:

Notes:

Place Name:

Location:

Date:

Notes:

Place Name:

Location:

Date:

Notes:

Place Name:

Location:

Date:

Notes:

MY
MEMORIES

MY MEMORIES

MY MEMORIES

MY MEMORIES

HIDDEN COTTAGE

PRESS

Made in the USA
Monee, IL
27 March 2022

93617728R10085